MW00679851

innocence

innocence

UNIVERSAL EXPRESSIONS OF CHILDHOOD

by victoria davis

WILLOW CREEK PRESS

Minocqua, Wisconsin

© 2000 by Willow Creek Press
Photographs © Victoria Davis

Published by Willow Creek Press
P.O. Box 147, Minocqua, Wisconsin 54548

For information on other Willow Creek Press titles, call 1-800-850-9453

Library of Congress Cataloging-in-Publication Data

Printed in Hong Kong

Believe in your dreams.

Acknowledgments

Where do I begin? First, and foremost, I'd like to thank all of the beautiful children. Without them and their wonderful parents this project would not be possible. They are my true inspiration. My friends and family, for always believing in me and putting up with me and my ideas which I'm constantly bouncing off of them. Cyja, Raquel, Jennifer, Karen, Daniela, Jenny, Amy, Kate, Toi, Patti & Rafe, Kathleen— you guys are the best. Andrea . . . thank you for always listening. My translators: Emiko, Daniela, Sonia, Valerie, Mary and Giselle. Thank you so much. My daughter, who is only 4 years old, thank you for your patience while mommy is constantly running to the labs and having new children in the house. And, of course, my parents . . . You are my backbone. You have given me the wings to fly.

For my beautiful daughter, Savannah.
You are my true inspiration
And for my parents
Thank you for always believing in me.
This is for you.

dreamy

soñadora

verträumt

rêveur

夢

precious

preciosa

kostbar

précieuse

親愛

gentle

gentil

sanftmütig

gentille

優しい

happy

feliz

froh

heureux

幸福

sad

triste

traurig

triste

悲しみ

shy

tímida

scheu

timide

内気

confident

....

segura

....

überzeugt

....

confiant

....

自信

soft

....

blanda

....

weich

....

douce

....

優しい

worried

....

preocupado

....

gesorgt

....

tourmenté

....

心配

adorable

---

adorable

---

bezaubernd

---

adorable

かわいい

cute

. . . .

listo

. . . .

reizeud

. . . .

rusé

. . . .

可愛い

playful

juguetón

spielerisch

le joueur

陽気

squeezable

apretable

knuddelig

embrassable

愛らしさ

cozy

cómodos

gemütlich

commode

温もり

charming

---

encantador

---

entzückend

---

charmant

魅力

tender

tierna

zart

tendre

柔らか

sneaky

furtivo

schlau

sécréteur

やんちゃ

defiant

desafiante

trotzig

défi

挑戦

bored

---

aburrida

---

angebohrt

---

n'intéresse

退屈

angelic

angélical

engelhaft

angélique

天使

pure

puro

rein

pur

純粋

spicy

....

picante

....

würzig

....

épicé

....

スパイシー

warm

caluroso

warm

chaud

優しさ

beautiful

bella

schön

belle

美

mischievious

traviesa

schelmisch

espiègle

悪戯

curious

curioso

neugierig

curieux

好奇心

contemplative

pondera

nachdenkend

contemplatif

思案

timeless

etermo

zeitlos

éternal

永遠

peaceful

pacifica

einträchtig

serein

穏やか

simple

....

sencillo

....

einfach

....

simple

....

素朴

joyful

---

alegre

---

freudig

---

joyeux

喜び

love

....

amor

....

Lieben

....

amour

....

sharing

compartiendo

teilnehmend

partageant

仲良し

loyalty

---

lealtad

Treue

---

loyauté

誠実

togetherness

compañerismo

die Zweisamkeit

ensemble

家族

laughter

....

risos

....

Lachen

....

rire

....

微笑み

sparkle

chispa

funkelnd

éclat

輝き

giving

generoso

selbstlos

généreux

与える

excitement

----

excitación

----

aufregung

----

excitation

興奮

friends

amigas

Freunde

les amies

友達

sweetness

dulzura

Suessigkeit

douceur

愛らしさ

trouble

---

afección

Schwierigkeit

---

trouble

いたずら

surprise

---

sorpreso

Überraschung

---

surpris

驚き

spirit

---

espíritu

Geist

---

esprit

明朗